Peach Girl

by Miwa Ueda

4

TOKYOPOP®

TOKYOPOP® Presents
Peach Girl 4 by Miwa Ueda
TOKYOPOP is a registered trademark
of Mixx Entertainment, Inc.
ISBN: 1-931514-14-3
First Printing May 2002

10 9 8 7 6 5 4 3 2

This volume contains the Peach Girl installments
from SMILE Magazine issues 4.2-4.5 in their entirety.

Translator - Dan Papia. Retouch Artist - Jinky De Leon.
Graphic Designer - Akemi Imafuku. Graphic Assistants - Raseel El-Djoundi and Dolly Chan.
Assistant Editors - Paul Morrissey and Trisha Kunimoto.
Editor - Robert Coyner. Senior Editor - Jake Forbes. Production Manager - Fred Lui.
Art Director - Matt Alford. Brand Manager - Kimberly J. Bird.
VP of Production - Ron Klamert. Publisher - Stuart Levy.

Email: editor@TOKYOPOP.com
Come visit us at www.TOKYOPOP.com

TOKYOPOP®
Los Angeles - Tokyo

I JUST CAN'T STAY TOGETHER WITH YOU, TOJI.

Peach Girl
by Miwa Ueda

BETWEEN MOMO AND LOVE, THERE IS SAE.

MOMO DIDN'T HAVE IT EASY. HER PAL, SAE, WAS A SNEAK THAT GOT KICKS BY PUTTING HER FRIENDS DOWN. AND MOMO'S BIGGEST FAN, THE CUTE BUT WILEY KILEY, STOLE MOMO'S FIRST KISS BEFORE SHE COULD GIVE IT TO HER TRUE LOVE, TOJI, THE BOY SHE'S HAD HER SIGHTS ON SINCE JR. HIGH BUT WAS TOO NERVOUS TO APPROACH BECAUSE HE SUPPOSEDLY DIDN'T LIKE DARK-SKINNED GIRLS. MOMO AND TOJI GOT TOGETHER AND HAD A FEW HAPPY DAYS, BUT SAE CREATED MISTRUTHS AND MISUNDERSTANDINGS THAT LED THE WHOLE SCHOOL TO TURN AGAINST MOMO AND MADE EVEN HER BELOVED TOJI DOUBT HER. THEN SAE TOLD EVERYONE MOMO WAS AN EXCELLENT SWIMMER AND HER CLASS DECIDED TO PUNISH HER BY SIGNING HER UP FOR EVERY EVENT IN THE SWIM MEET. KILEY CAME THROUGH IN THE END, SEEING TO IT THAT SAE WAS OUT AND MOMO REDEEMED. BUT WHEN TOJI SUGGESTED THEY GIVE IT ANOTHER TRY, MOMO REFUSED. IF HE DOUBTED HER ONCE, HOW CAN SHE KNOW HE WON'T DO IT AGAIN?

SUMMARY OF WHAT'S GOING ON

MOMO ADACHI STRAIGHT AND HONEST, BUT HER LIGHT HAIR AND DARK SKIN MAKE HER LOOK LIKE A BIMBO.

KILEY OKAYASU HE'S GOT HIS SHARE OF FEMALE FANS, BUT HE LIKES MOMO. AND HE WAS HER FIRST KISS.

KAZUYA TOJIGAMORI EVERYONE CALLS HIM TOJI. HE'S A LITTLE SHY BUT STRONG AND GOOD-HEARTED.

SAE KASHIWAGI WATCH OUT FOR THIS ONE. SHE'LL DESTROY YOU AND THE BOYS WILL TAKE HER SIDE.

CON-GRATS TO CLASS THREE!
YOU'VE ALL WON A VICTORY KARAOKE PARTY!
FREE FOOD AND DRINKS FOR EVERYONE, COMPLIMENTS OF THE STUDENT ASSOCIATION!
VICTORY
CLAP
CLAP
CLAP
CLAP
HOORAY!
TA-DA!
AH!
WAIT A MINUTE. THIS IS CAFETERIA FOOD!
THOUGH THE SELECTION IS BETTER THAN USUAL.
THIS IS OUR KARAOKE PARTY?
THAT'S JUST THE BOOM BOX FROM THE TEACHERS' LOUNGE.
I THOUGH' IT WAS TOO GOOD TO BE TRUE.
WHAT THE...?!

OH, WELL. AS LONG AS EVERYONE'S HAVING A GOOD TIME.
EVERY-ONE, LET'S HEAR IT FOR OUR CHAMP.
HOORAY!
CLAP
CLAP
CLAP
HEY, PASS THE MIC.
THAT'S RIGHT. SHE CARRIED US ALMOST SINGLE-HANDED-LY.
AND IT'S ALL THANKS TO MOMO.
ALREADY TALKING LIKE THEY'RE OLD PALS!
CLAP CLAP
CLAP CLAP
NO, I...
I MEAN, IT WAS...

HEY, TOJI.
COME WATCH WHILE WE GET OUR LICKS FROM MOMO.
NO, I DON'T ...
MAN, DON'T BE LIKE THAT. CHECK IT OUT.
WE'RE SORRY, MOMO.
PLEASE FORGIVE US.
WE WERE IDIOTS.
COME ON, HIT US WITH THIS UNTIL YOU FEEL BETTER.

THAT'S ALRIGHT.

I CAN SEE YOU GUYS ARE SORRY.

I'M OVER IT. REALLY.

YOU'RE BEING WAY TOO NICE!

DON'T YOU REMEMBER WHAT THEY DID TO YOU? THE WAY THEY ALL SNUBBED YOU?

I MEAN, UH...

THE WAY WE ALL TREAT-ED YOU.

I WAS MEAN TO YOU TOO, MOMO. I'M SORRY.

YOU CAN SMACK ME TOO.

NOW THAT I THINK ABOUT IT, YOU GUYS DID SOAK MY CLOTHES IN WATER.

GULP

AND YOU CUT THE STRAPS ON MY SWIM-SUIT.

GULP

SHIVER

SHIVER

H-HIT US...

WE DE-SERVE IT.

SHIVER SHIVER

OH, MOMO! YOU'RE JUST SO...SO....
I FORGIVE YOU.
WELL, YOU ALL SEEM TO REGRET WHAT YOU'VE DONE. I GUESS THAT MEANS YOU'RE ALREADY PAYING FOR IT.
HEY, TOJI'S HERE!
!

TOJI AND MOMO!
THEY'RE BACK TOGETHER!
WHIRL
yay

UH OH, LOOKS LIKE THEY'RE EMBAR-RASSED.
TEE-HEE
TOJI'S A SHY ONE.
WE SHOULD HAVE REALIZED THEY WERE A COUPLE.
THEN NONE OF THIS WOULD HAVE HAPPENED.
.....
RIGHT, BUT HOW WERE WE SUPPOSED TO KNOW WHAT A LIAR SAE WAS?
CHITTER
CHATTER
YEAH, WHAT A SHOCK.
GUESS YOU NEVER CAN TELL.
OF COURSE, LOTS OF US WERE SUSPICIOUS OF SAE FROM THE GET-GO.
OH, RIGHT. LIKE THE WAY SHE'D TOTALLY CHANGE WHENEVER A GUY WAS AROUND.
SUDDENLY, SHE'D BE ALL CHARMING.
I'VE NEVER HEARD ANYONE SAY THAT BEFORE.
'CAUSE IF WE DID, YOU'D JUST CALL IT JEALOUSY BECAUSE SAE'S SO CUTE.

GUYS CAN BE TOTALLY TAKEN IN BY A CUTE GIRL.
NO KIDDING!
?!
FLIP
FLAP
HA HA HA
BET HER EGO'S REALLY BEEN DEFLATED.
HMMM?
SPEAKING OF WHICH, WHERE IS SAE?
MAYBE SHE WENT HOME?

HOORAY! YA

WAS THAT ...?
WAS SAE JUST HERE?
BA-BUMP
BA-BUMP
BA-BUMP
SAE? YOU MUST BE IMAG-INING THINGS.
DID YOU SEE HER? I DIDN'T SEE HER.

TOJI, WHY DON'T YOU SING ONE TO CELEBRATE GETTING OUT OF THE HOS-PITAL?
WHAT?
COME ON, DO A DUET WITH MOMO.
WAIT ...
DUET! DUET!
THERE'S ONLY ONE MICROPHONE, BUT YOU TWO SHOULDN'T MIND GETTING CLOSE.♡
COME ON YOU TWO. GIVE US A SMILE.
CLI-CLICK
PUT YOUR ARM AROUND HER, TOJI!
CLOSER! WE CAN'T HEAR!
LIKE EARLIER TODAY WHEN YOU ANNOUNCED SHE WAS YOUR GIRL-FRIEND.
WILL YOU ALL BACK OFF?

HUH? WHERE'S SHE...?
I'M SORRY. EXCUSE ME.
.....
BUT I WAS JUST...
TOLD YOU SHE'S SHY. YOU SHOULDN'T EMBARRASS HER LIKE THAT.

NURSE'S OFFICE

SIGH

I'VE LOST HER.

NURSE MISAO, I NEED CONSOL-ING.

GRRRR

I'M BUSY.

I'M DEPRESSED. I NEED COMFORTING!!!
HELP ME!
HELP ME!
SNAP
I'M WORK-ING!

...
SIGH
AW, CRUD.
SNIFFLE SNIFFLE
SEEMS THIS ONE WAS FOR REAL, HUH?
POOR LITTLE GUY.
SNIFF
SNIFF SNIFF
.....
SNIFF SNIFFLE
CLANK
OWWWW
cold-hearted wench ...
WELL, IF YOU'RE HEALTHY ENOUGH TO CRACK JOKES, I GUESS YOU'LL SURVIVE.
TAP
TAP
LEAP
THAT'S OKAY. I'M FINE. YOU'VE ALWAYS BEEN MY ONE TRUE LOVE. ♡

OH, WELL.
HEY, MO--
SMACK
SWALLOW
CAN'T DO IT. CAN'T DO IT.
Got to watch myself before I slip back to my old ways.
tip toe
tip toe
I'LL JUST TAKE ANOTHER ROUTE.
Stop. Not here.
Come on, just a little kiss.
GRRR.
HEY, KILEY !
!!

I... UH...
OH, HI, MOMO. WHAT ARE YOU DOING HERE?
I THOUGHT YOU WERE AT THAT VICTORY PARTY IN THE CAFETERIA.
......
BUT I HAD TO LEAVE.
I WAS.
NOTHING'S EVER EASY.
WELL, I GUESS TOJI'S AROUND HERE SOMEWHERE, EH? WHERE IS HE?
I SEE.
...
BUT THINGS ARE GOING GOOD BETWEEN YOU AND TOJI, RIGHT?
WHAT?
HE'S NOT HERE, KILEY. I'M ALONE.

BUT I HAD TO SAY NO.
HE ASKED ME TO GET BACK TOGETHER WITH HIM.

WELL... I...
ARE YOU CRAZY?! SAE'S OUT OF YOUR LIFE.
THE BOY OF YOUR DREAMS WANTS YOU BACK AND YOU SAY "NO"?!
YIKES!
YOU WHAT ?!
DON'T FLATTER YOURSELF! I JUST DON'T KNOW HOW I CAN TRUST HIM AFTER WHAT HAPPENED.
SO WHAT'S THE DEAL? YOU'RE NOT GOING TO SAY IT'S BECAUSE YOU HAVE FEELINGS FOR ME, ARE YOU?
HOW DARE HE? WHAT AN ARROGANT LUNK HEAD.
The one saving grace was that when he said it i agreed...
AND NOW THAT I THINK ABOUT IT,
AFTER ALL, IT WAS BASICALLY TOJI WHO SUGGESTED WE BREAK UP.
HOW DO I KNOW HE'S NOT GOING TO START DOUBTING ME AGAIN THE FIRST CHANCE HE GETS?
IF TOJI'S THE TYPE OF PERSON WHO COULD BELIEVE SO EASILY ALL THOSE THINGS THAT SAE SAID,
You could have just said, "yes, Kiley, I have feelings for you..."
BUMP
LET GO OF ME. I'M NOT DRUNK.
COME ON, MAN, STRAIGHTEN UP. YOU'RE ZONKED.

HUH?
WOW, LOOK AT THIS TANNED LITTLE CUTIE. ♡
What breath!
HOW ABOUT IT, SWEETIE? ARE YOU THE TYPE THAT LIKES TO PARTY WITH OLDER MEN?
I'LL GIVE YOU THREE-HUNDRED FOR THE WHOLE NIGHT.
?!
EH?
WHERE'D THAT LITTLE PUNK COME FROM?
COME ON, MAN, YOU'RE WASTED. LET'S GO.
EXCUSE US, MISS. I'M REAL SORRY.
WHAT ARE YOU APOLOGIZING TO THEM FOR? SHE'S OBVIOUSLY A PLAYGIRL. JUST LOOK AT HER.
Nice girls don't get tans like that. She's sun-roasted.
Quit embarrassing us.
....

T-H-A-T BURNS ME UP!
THOSE OLD CREEPS. THE NERVE!
ASSUMING THAT I'D GO OUT WITH THEM FOR ANY AMOUNT OF MONEY--!
YEAH, SOME NERVE. BUT THE PART ABOUT YOU BEING SUN-ROASTED IS TRUE.
LOOK HOW TAN YOUR FACE GOT!
I KNEW IT! THIS ALWAYS HAPPENS WHEN I GO SWIMMING!
MY FACE IS COOKED!
I CAN'T STAND IT. I NEVER GET RED, JUST DARK.
THANK GOODNESS YOU WERE HERE.
SIGH
OH, MY FACE HURTS...
BECAUSE YOU GOT BURNED, RIGHT?
IF I HADN'T BEEN WITH A GUY LIKE YOU, WHO KNOWS WHAT MIGHT HAVE HAPPENED?
HEY, THAT'S RIGHT. THE SAME THING HAPPENED LAST TIME, TOO.
IF I HADN'T BEEN THERE, THAT OLD MAN MIGHT HAVE DRAGGED YOU INTO THAT HOTEL.
AARRGGHH
DON'T REMIND ME!!
BUT HE'S GOT A POINT. HE'S SAVED ME TWICE NOW.
MOMO? REMEMBER WHAT I SAID THAT TIME?

THAT COOL LINE I GAVE THE OLD MAN.
HUH?
OH, YEAH.
"SHE MAY NOT LOOK IT AT FIRST GLANCE, BUT MOMO IS DEFINITELY NOT THAT KIND OF GIRL."
OF COURSE I REMEMBER.
THAT WAS THE MOMENT I BEGAN TO SEE KILEY IN A NEW LIGHT.
YOU KNOW, KILEY, YOU MAY BE A PERVERT, BUT AT LEAST YOU DON'T RUSH TO JUDGE PEOPLE.
THAT'S ONE THING I RESPECT ABOUT YOU.
THA-THANKS, BUT YOU SEE...
THAT WASN'T MY LINE. IT WAS TOJI'S.
SHOOT. NOW IT'S GOING TO BE TWICE AS HARD TO SAY...

TOJI'S ?!
SCRATCH SCRATCH
WELL, YEAH. YOU SEE...
...IT WAS BEFORE YOU AND TOJI WERE GOING OUT.
TOJI HAD HEARD THAT RUMOR ABOUT YOU AND I KISSING.
HE GRABBED ME BY THE SHIRT AND WARNED ME...
YOU STAY AWAY FROM MOMO!
GULP
AND THAT'S WHEN HE GAVE ME THE LINE ABOUT FIRST GLANCES BEING DECEPTIVE. ♡
I THOUGHT IT SOUNDED COOL, SO I BORROWED IT.
IT PROBABLY TOOK SAE A LONG TIME TO GET HIM TO THINK THAT WAY.
SO DON'T BELIEVE HE DOUBTED YOU THAT EASILY.
THAT'S HOW WELL TOJI UNDERSTANDS YOU.

SAE LED TOJI INTO A MAZE. SHE GOT HIM TO A PLACE WHERE HE COULDN'T SEE THE REAL YOU ANYMORE.
AND TODAY, TOJI FINALLY FOUND HIS WAY OUT OF THAT MAZE.
HE MUST HAVE DANDRUFF...
AT LEAST, THAT'S HOW IT SEEMS TO ME. NOT THAT I REALLY WANT TO BE HELPING HIM.

NO. THE DAY HE STOPPED TRUSTING ME, I LOST SOMETHING I CAN NEVER GET BACK.
IF I GET BACK TOGETHER WITH TOJI, HOW CAN I BE SURE THAT THE NEXT TIME SOMETHING HAPPENS, HE WON'T DOUBT ME AGAIN?
NO...
WAIT A MINUTE...
ARE YOU SURE THAT'S WHY YOU WON'T...
I MEAN, IT'S NOT LIKE THE REAL REASON IS BECAUSE...?
I JUST TOLD YOU.

DO YOU HAVE SAND IN YOUR EARS?
THAT'S WHY YOU WON'T MAKE UP WITH TOJI?
YOU'RE SURE?
IF THAT'S YOUR REASON, IT'S HORRIBLE.
MOMO, PLEASE.
HOW CA I MAKE SURE HE WON'T D THE SAM THING AGAIN?
WHAT DO YOU MEAN?
HOW ABOU THAT NOTHIN CERTA
POOR TOJI. I CAN'T HELP BUT FEEL SORRY FOR HIM.

WHAT GOOD DOES IT DO TO DENY YOURSELF WHAT YOU WANT JUST BECAUSE YOU'RE AFRAID OF WHAT MIGHT HAPPEN IN THE FUTURE?
THAT'S LIKE NEVER LEAVING THE HOUSE BECAUSE YOU MIGHT GET IN AN ACCIDENT OUTSIDE.
LISTEN TO YOURSELF: "THE DAY HE STOPPED TRUSTING ME, I LOST SOMETHING I CAN NEVER GET BACK."
DO YOU REALLY MEAN THAT?
IT SOUNDS LIKE THE ONE WHO DOESN'T HAVE ANY TRUST ISN'T TOJI. IT'S YOU.

IT'S JUST TOO STUPID. I GIVE UP.
YOU'VE DECIDED THAT IT'S NEVER GOING TO WORK OUT AND YOU'RE MAKING IT ALL TOJI'S FAULT.
WITH THAT ATTITUDE, YOU'LL NEVER FIND SOMEONE.

ALL STUDENTS, PROCEED TO THE GYMNASIUM.
WILL ALL STUDENTS PLEASE REPORT TO THE GYMNASIUM.
CHITTER CHATTER
IF MY GRADES GO DOWN, I'M IN TROUBLE.
CHITTER CHATTER
YEAH, BUT WHAT ARE WE GOING TO DO AFTER TODAY?
WOW! THAT'S COOL.
THAT'S RIGHT, FOUR DAYS.
NO WAY!
GUAM?!

KILEY'S A BIG PAIN IN THE BUTT, BUT HE'S ALSO RIGHT.

HE ALWAYS SEEMS TO POINT OUT THINGS I DON'T WANT TO ADMIT. I HATE THAT.

YOU'VE DECIDED THAT IT'S NEVER GOING TO WORK OUT AND YOU'RE MAKING IT ALL TOJI'S FAULT.

I GUESS I'VE ALWAYS HAD THIS COMPLEX.

I WONDER HOW LONG I'VE BEEN LIKE THIS.

"A PLAYGIRL." "A BEACH BUNNY." "LOOSE AND EASY."

EVERYONE JUMPS TO CONCLUSIONS. NO ONE KNOWS THE REAL ME.

THE WAY PEOPLE JUDGE ME BECAUSE OF MY DARK SKIN.

THE WAY THEY STARE.

TOJI WAS QUICK TO DISTRUST ME BECAUSE MY SKIN IS TANNED.

HE DOUBTED ME BECAUSE HE'S JUST ANOTHER JERK.

SINCE THIS ALWAYS HAPPENS, IT'S HARD TO TRUST HIM AGAIN.

I DON'T THINK I CAN EVER FEEL THE SAME AGAIN.

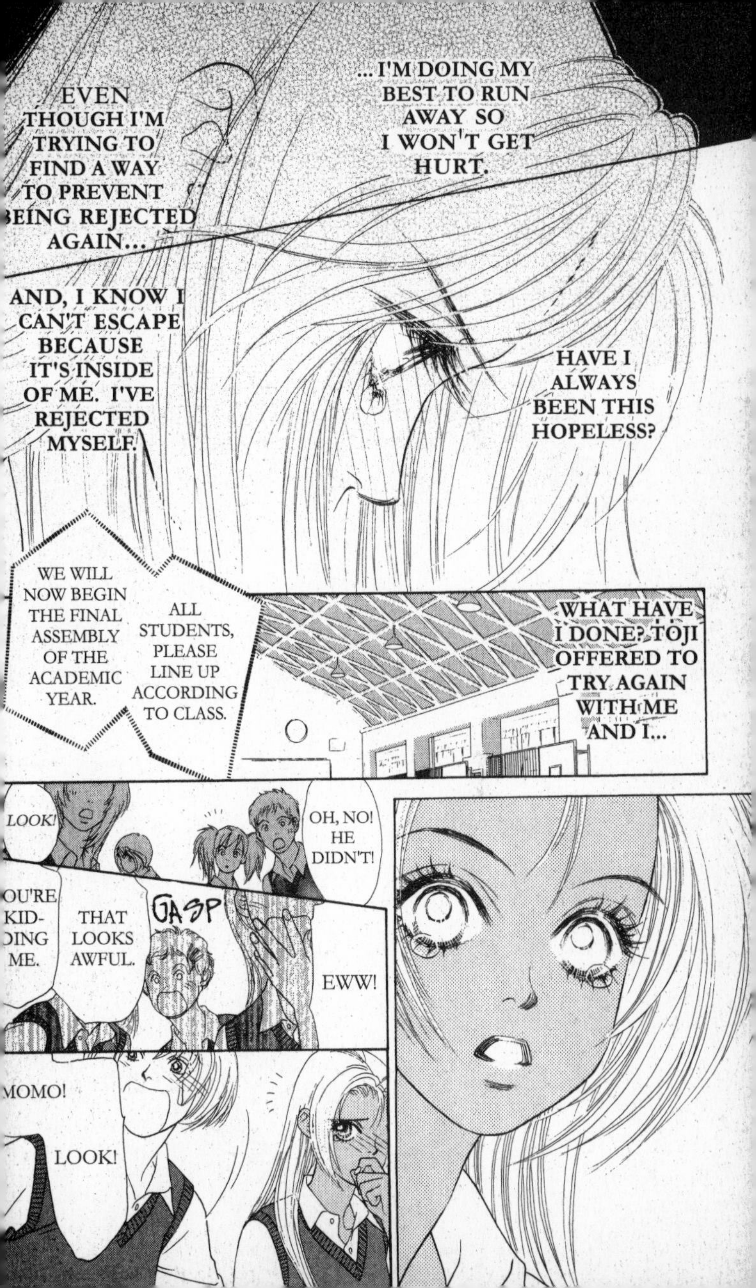
...I'M DOING MY BEST TO RUN AWAY SO I WON'T GET HURT.
EVEN THOUGH I'M TRYING TO FIND A WAY TO PREVENT BEING REJECTED AGAIN...
HAVE I ALWAYS BEEN THIS HOPELESS?
AND, I KNOW I CAN'T ESCAPE BECAUSE IT'S INSIDE OF ME. I'VE REJECTED MYSELF.
WHAT HAVE I DONE? TOJI OFFERED TO TRY AGAIN WITH ME AND I...
ALL STUDENTS, PLEASE LINE UP ACCORDING TO CLASS.
WE WILL NOW BEGIN THE FINAL ASSEMBLY OF THE ACADEMIC YEAR.
OH, NO! HE DIDN'T!
LOOK!
EWW!
GASP
THAT LOOKS AWFUL.
OU'RE KID-DING ME.
MOMO!
LOOK!

TOJI...
CHITTER
CHATTER
QUICKLY, STUDENTS. TAKE YOUR PLACES.
QUIET, EVERY-ONE.
SHUFFLE
SHUFFLE
SHUFFLE
CLAMOR

CHITTER
YOU THINK IT'S THA TRADITI ABOUT CUTTIN YOUR HA WHEN YO HEART BROKE
THAT BUZZ CUT DOESN'T SUIT HIM AT ALL.
.....
CHATTER
ABSO-LUTELY INCRED-IBLE.
CHITTER
SIMPLY TRAGIC. THE STATE HE MUST BE IN!
OH ...
WHY DON'T THEY ALL SHUT UP?
COULD IT BE BECAUSE OF WHAT I SAID TO HIM YES-TERDAY?
HEY, TOJI!
GRUMBLE
MUMBLE
CHATTER
CHITTER

BRUSH
BRUSH
.....
I JUST DECIDED...
...I DIDN'T WANT TO STAND OUT.
TOJI... WHY?

I DIDN'T DO IT TO GET YOUR ATTENTION OR ANYTHING LIKE THAT.
BUT I DIDN'T MEAN TO...
MAYBE I SHOULD HAVE WAITED ONE MORE DAY.
....
...
I'M SORRY, MOMO.
WE WERE SO LUCKY TO HAVE COME TOGETHER...
...AND I THREW IT ALL AWAY.

I GUESS KILEY WAS RIGHT.
I'M TOO GULLIBLE AND BELIEVE WHATEVER I'M TOLD.
YOU'RE NOT VERY WORLDLY, ARE YOU?
YOU JUST TAKE WHAT PEOPLE SAY AT FACE VALUE.
... I SWALLOWED ALL THAT GARBAGE THAT SAE FED ME ABOUT YOU.
EVEN THOUGH I NEVER SAW IT OR HEARD IT MYSELF ...
AND BECAUSE I WAS SUCH A DOPE...
...I CAUSED YOU ALL THAT PAIN.
I'M SORRY, MOMO.

WELL, I'LL SEE YOU AROUND.

TOJI! WAIT!!
SAE LED HIM INTO A MAZE. SHE GOT TOJI TO A PLACE WHERE HE COULDN'T SEE THE REAL YOU ANYMORE.

I'VE COMPLETELY IGNORED YOUR FEELINGS.
I'M SO SORRY, TOJI. I'VE JUST BEEN MAKING MYSELF THE VICTIM IN MY OWN MIND.
.....
SO SHOCKED HE'S SPEECHLESS.
FORGIVE ME.

I MEAN, YES, YOU MAY BE A LITTLE SLOW SOMETIMES.
AND STUBBORN. AND SELFISH. AND UNABLE TO SEE THE TRUTH. AND SOMETIMES YOU MAKE ME THINK, "WHAT A BLOCKHEAD."
SQUEEEEEZZZEEEE
BUT STILL ...
......
... THOSE ARE A LOT OF THE THINGS THAT ATTRACTED ME TO YOU IN THE FIRST PLACE.
AND EVEN NOW, I STILL WANT TO BE WITH YOU.

YOU'RE FINE.
I'M JUST...
B-BUT I, I MEAN, LOOK AT ME.
THE TOJI THAT I'M WITH RIGHT NOW ...
THIS TOJI THAT'S BEEN TORTURING HIMSELF BECAUSE HE REGRETS THE WAY HE MADE ME FEEL...
THIS IS THE TOJI I LOVE.

DO YOU THINK WE COULD GIVE IT ONE MORE CHANCE?

IT WAS THE FIRST SUMMER VACATION THAT I EVER HAD A BOYFRIEND TO ENJOY IT WITH.

THE TIME WENT BY TOO QUICKLY, LIKE THE FLASH OF FIREWORKS FADING INTO NIGHT.

THE NEW SCHOOL YEAR

GIGGLE

JIGGLE JIGGLE

GIGGLE

TEE HEE HEE

COME ON, MOMO.
SCRATCH
SCRATCH
....
I CAN'T RESIST. IT FEELS SO GOOD. ♡
tee hee
I GUESS IT'S PART OF THE PACKAGE.
DO YOU HAVE TO RUB MY HAIR EVERY TIME I SEE YOU?
DING DONG
THINGS RETURNED TO THE WAY THEY ONCE HAD BEEN.
A MONTH AND TEN DAYS SINCE TOJI AND I GOT BACK, TOGETHER.
YOU DON'T FEEL LIKE CUTTING IT REAL SHORT AGAIN FOR ME, DO YOU?
OF COURSE, IT DOESN'T FEEL NEARLY AS NICE NOW AS IT DID WHEN YOU FIRST GOT THE BUZZ CUT.
NO, I DON'T.
DING DONG
OH, NO!
IT'S TIME

A LOT HAPPENED BEFORE WE EVER GOT HERE.

BUT NOW WE'RE FINALLY HAPPY.

SO HOT YOU WERE SMOKIN
YOU SLY FOX!
LITTLE MINX!
YOU TWO HOLDING HANDS ALL MORNING.
SOME-ONE CLEARLY ENJOYED THEIR SUMMER
WE SAW IT ALL, MOMO.
UH OH
?!
YOU CAN TELL US, MOMO. HOW FAR DID YOU LET HIM GO? ♡
TITTER LEER
......
GIGGLE GIGGLE
WHAT? YOU MEAN YOU DIDN'T DO ANYTHING?!

WELL, AFTER ALL, HE'D JUST GOTTEN OUT OF THE HOSPITAL. AND THEN HE HAD STUDIES TO DO OVER THE SUMMER.
ALL WE HAD TIME FOR WAS TO GET TOGETHER AFTER HIS CLASSES AND MAYBE GO TO THE LIBRARY TO STUDY.
THEN IF WE WERE LUCKY, WE'D SEE A MOVIE. OR MAYBE GO TO THE GAME CENTER.
THAT'S ALL?
OH NO, WAIT.
WE DID GO TO WATCH FIREWORKS ONCE.
HOW ABOUT GOING AWAY ON A TRIP, JUST THE TWO OF YOU?
OF COURSE NOT.
HOW COULD WE DO THAT?!
WHAT A GYP!
YEAH RIGHT, MOMO WHO ARE YOU KIDDING?
WHAT'S THE USE?
SHE DOESN'T WANT TO TELL. I THINK IT'S CUTE.
HA HA HA HA HA
HEE HEE HEE.
ALL WE HAVE TO DO IS LOOK TO SEE THAT THERE'S MORE GOING ON.

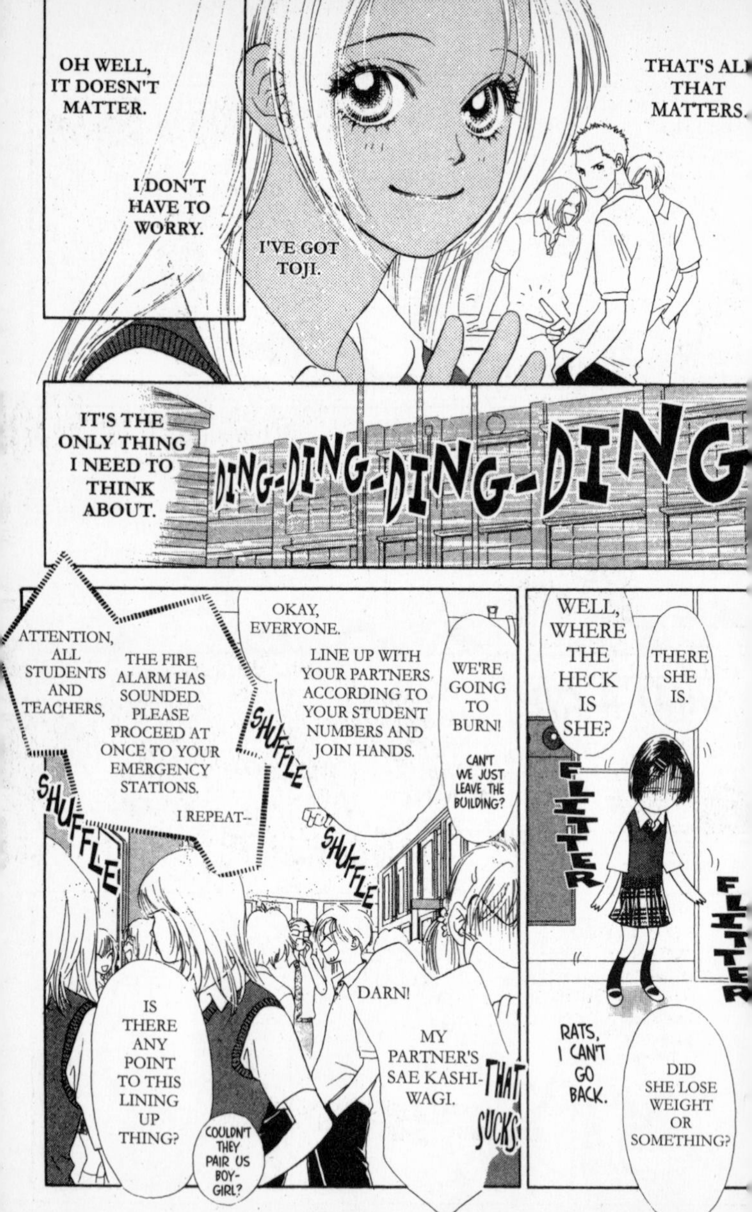
OH WELL, IT DOESN'T MATTER.
I DON'T HAVE TO WORRY.
I'VE GOT TOJI.
THAT'S ALL THAT MATTERS.
IT'S THE ONLY THING I NEED TO THINK ABOUT.
DING-DING-DING-DING
ATTENTION, ALL STUDENTS AND TEACHERS,
THE FIRE ALARM HAS SOUNDED. PLEASE PROCEED AT ONCE TO YOUR EMERGENCY STATIONS.
I REPEAT--
SHUFFLE
SHUFFLE
SHUFFLE
OKAY, EVERYONE.
LINE UP WITH YOUR PARTNERS ACCORDING TO YOUR STUDENT NUMBERS AND JOIN HANDS.
WE'RE GOING TO BURN!
CAN'T WE JUST LEAVE THE BUILDING?
IS THERE ANY POINT TO THIS LINING UP THING?
COULDN'T THEY PAIR US BOY-GIRL?
DARN!
MY PARTNER'S SAE KASHI-WAGI.
THAT SUCKS!
WELL, WHERE THE HECK IS SHE?
THERE SHE IS.
FLITTER
FLITTER
RATS, I CAN'T GO BACK.
DID SHE LOSE WEIGHT OR SOMETHING?

DO I REALLY HAVE TO HOLD HER HAND?
DON'T WORRY ABOUT IT. OUR CLASS HAS AN EXTRA GIRL, ANYWAY.
THAT MAKES SENSE.
AL-RIGHT. EVERY-BODY OUT.
SPRAY
RATTLE RATTLE
BOOM BOOM BOOM
FLITTER FLATTER
FLITTER FLATTER
STEP ASIDE! QUICK!
1-5
1-5
HURRY UP! OUT OF THE WAY!
BOOM BOOM BOO
POINK
FLITTER FLATTER
SMACK
CRACKL
SOMETIMES, WHEN YOU'VE TAKEN TOO MUCH, YOU JUST DON'T HAVE ANYTHING LEFT TO FIGHT BACK WITH.

CLICK CLACK
DING DONG
DING DONG
CLICK CLACK
CLICK CLACK
BAM
1-3
WE'RE LOOKING FOR MOMO ADACHI. IS SHE IN THIS CLASS?

WHAT DID YOU DO TO THEM, MOMO?
THOSE GIRLS ARE 11TH GRADERS.
I DIDN'T DO ANY-THING.
DIDN'T YOU USE TO BE ON THE SWIM TEAM?
AND AREN'T YOU THE ONE THAT SINGLE-HANDEDLY WON THE SWIM MEET?
I HEARD THE PARTY WAS REAL NICE.
DO YOU THINK WE'RE GOING TO STAND BY AND WATCH A RINGER CREAM US IN EVERY EVENT?
UH OH. SOUNDS LIKE THEY'VE COME TO COMPLAIN.
BUT SHE DIDN'T DO ANYTHING WRONG. THERE'S NOTHING IN THE RULES THAT SAYS HOW MANY EVENTS YOU CAN ENTER.
!!
SMACK

PLEASE, MOMO, YOU'VE GOT TO HELP US!
HUH ?
IT HAD SEVEN MEMBERS, BUT THREE OF THEM JUS GRADUATED AND NOW THEY'RE GOING TO GET SHUT DOWN UNLESS I JOIN.
I DIDN'T EVEN KNOW OUR SCHOOL HAD ONE OF THOSE.
SIGH
THEY PLEADED WITH ME FOR OVER AN HOUR.
THE SWIM TEAM BOOST-ER SQUAD ?

IF I DID THAT, I WOULDN'T HAVE A CHANCE!!!
PLUS, WHAT WILL PEOPLE THINK IF I START HANGING AROUND WITH THE LIKES OF THEM?
FOR ONE THING, I DON'T NEED TO GET ANY TANNER THAN I ALREADY AM.
SO, WHY DON'T YOU SIGN UP?
AND LAUGHING WHEN YOU TALK TO PEOPLE?
WHY DON'T YOU TRY SMILING
OKAY, I'VE GOT AN IDEA.
PEOPLE WOULD THINK YOU WERE A BAD GIRL.
WELL, I GUESS IF YOU JOINED THAT BUNCH,
WE'RE THE FOUR TAN BABES THAT LOVE SWIMMERS AND SWIMMING. DON'T MESS WITH US.
THAT'S WHAT I MEAN.
NO, I DIDN'T MEAN TO SAY THAT YOU HAD A MEAN FACE I MEANT...
ARE YOU SAYING I HAVE A "MEAN FACE"?
IT JUST LIGHTENS THE AIR.
I MEAN, EVEN THAT BALLPLAYER I KNOW. HE HAS A REALLY MEAN FACE, BUT WHEN HE SMILES...
IT REALLY MAKES A DIFFER-ENCE.
NO. WHAT I WAS TRYING TO SAY WAS...
YOU'RE THE MEAN ONE!

...THAT YOUR SMILE IS SO POWERFUL IT COULD COMFORT ANYONE.

HONESTLY...
I MEAN, YOU DO LIKE SWIMMING, DON'T YOU?
YES.
AND I DON'T CARE HOW TAN YOU GET. I'LL STILL LIKE YOU.
REALLY?
IT WAS NICE OF HIM TO SAY, BUT IT'S TOJI THAT HAS THE PRICELESS SMILE.
THANK YOU, TOJI. I'LL GO TALK TO THE CLUB PRESI-DENT.
ANYWAY, HOW 'BOUT A HUG?
WHAT?
!
HAI-YA!

NORMALLY, KILEY'S ALWAYS AROUND TO MAKE A PASS AT ME OR GET ON MY NERVES IN SOME OTHER WAY.
BUT COME TO THINK OF IT, I HAVEN'T SEEN HIM AT ALL TODAY.
REALLY? YOU'LL JOIN?
OH, THANK YOU!
WHOA
MOMO? WHAT ARE YOU DOING?
OH... ER...
UH...
NO-THING.
GULP
!!
THE WAY HE SAID THAT REMINDED ME OF KILEY.
PANT PANT
SHOULD I WONDER WHERE HE IS?
NO. HE'LL POP UP SOON ENOUGH.
MOMO? WHAT ARE YOU DOING?
IN FACT, I'LL BET HE'S--

YOO-HOO! KILEY! ♡
PROB-ABLY BEING CHASED BY GIRLS.
LET'S GO FIND HIM.
SAME OLD KILEY.
KILEY'S CLASSMATES
HE'S WANDER-ING AROUND SOME-WHERE, JUST LIKE HE ALWAYS DOES.
KILEY?
HA HA HA!
HEY, KILEY!
KILEY'S AVOIDING ME.
I SEE HE LET HIS HAIR GROW...
I GUESS IT'S TRUE.

HEY, KILEY WHA ABO ME
TEE HEE
MAYBE HE FINALLY GOT TIRED OF GOING THROUGH THE MOTIONS.
"I CAN'T GO OUT WITH YOU."
I DON'T NEED TO TORTURE MYSELF WITH ANY OF THIS. I'M HAPPY WITH TOJI
← SO SHE SAYS.
I'M SUCH AN IDIOT.
OR MAYBE HE WASN'T JUST GAGA FOR ME. HE HAS LOTS OF FISH ON HIS LINE.
GIRLS ROOM

ANOTHER ONE OF SAE'S "VICTIMS."
WE BOTH KNOW HOW IT FEELS.
ISN'T THAT SUMIRE, FROM CLASS ONE? THE GIRL WHO USED TO HAVE THE PONYTAIL?
SPLISH
SPLISH
HOW'S IT BEEN WITH SAE SINCE THEN?
"SINCE THEN?"
SHE'S BEEN AS QUIET
AS A KITTEN AWAY FROM HOME.
ALMOST LIKE SHE ISN'T THERE.
STRANGE, IN FACT...
IT WAS REALLY A GREAT COINCIDENCE THAT ALL HER VICTIMS HAPPENED TO BE THERE AT JUST THE RIGHT TIME.
TOTALLY.
ONCE THE SCHOOL FOUND HER OUT, THAT WAS IT.
ARE YOU SERIOUS?! YOU DON'T KNOW ?!
?

IT WAS NO COINCIDENCE. KILEY CALLED ME UP THE NIGHT BEFORE THE SWIM MEET.

"THIS IS KILEY FROM SCHOOL. I HEARD YOU HAD A PROBLEM WITH SAE A LONG TIME AGO."

"HOW'D YOU LIKE TO GET YOUR RE-VENGE?"

HE LOOKED UP MY NUMBER AND...

SAE PICKED ON ME WAY BACK IN JR. HIGH. I THOUGHT,

"WHY'S HE CALLING ME NOW?"

AFTER ALL, IT WAS THE FIRST TIME KILEY'D EVER TALKED TO ME.

BUT WHEN I SAW WHAT WAS HAPPENING TO YOU IN THE CAFETERIA, I FIGURED IT OUT.

SO, KILEY DIDN'T JUST DO IT FOR ME! HE DID IT FOR HER!

HELPING TO CLEAR THE AIR BETWEEN YOU AND TOJI WAS GREAT THERAPY FOR ME.
AND TO TOP IT OFF, KILEY AND I WENT OUT ON A DATE AFTERWARDS. HEY? MOMO?
THAT JERK!
I'M SO STUPID!
WHY WOULD I HAVE EVEN THOUGHT HE DID IT FOR ME?
"SMILE, MOMO."
"I'VE NEVER SEEN YOU HAPPIER THAN WHEN YOU WERE WITH TOJI."
I MEAN, I NEVER DID ANY-THING FOR HIM! BUT STILL...

I SHOULD HAVE KNOWN WHAT HE WAS DOING.

"I CAN'T BE THE ONE TO TAKE THAT HAPPY FACE AWAY."

ACTING SO SELFLESS ALL OF A SUDDEN. NOT LIKE THE TRUE KILEY AT ALL.

"HOW ABOUT A HUG?"

AND
THAT WAS
OUR LAST
EMBRACE...

KILEY!!!

PANT
PANT
PANT
HIYA.

I'M SORRY.
HUH ?
I'VE BEEN SPENDING ALL MY ENERGY WORRYING ABOUT MYSELF.
AND NOW THAT I THINK ABOUT IT, I HAVEN'T BEEN SEN-SITIVE TO YOUR NEEDS AT ALL.
...
WELL, WHEN YOU TOLD ME...
"HE ASKED ME TO GET TOGETHER WITH HIM,
BUT I DON'T KNOW. IF HE DIDN'T TRUST ME THEN, HOW DO I KNOW IF HE'LL EVER..."
I THOUGHT TO MYSELF,
"DANG, SHE OBVIOUSL CRAZY ABOU THE GUY.
I'VE GOT TO DO SOMETHIN
.....

I'M SORRY, KILEY.
CALM DOWN. DON'T GET ALL MIXED UP AGAIN. WHAT'S WRONG WITH YOU, ANYWAY?
....
SUMIRE TOLD ME.
SHE EXPLAINED WHAT YOU DID FOR ME. HOW YOU ARRANGED THINGS.
!
....

TO WORK OUT PERFECTLY AND YOU TWO GOT THAT MAGIC BACK.
AND WHAT DO YOU KNOW? IT ALL JUST HAP-PENED
YEAH, I SET A FEW THINGS UP WHILE TOJI WASN'T AROUND.
EH HEH.
YOU FOUND OUT, HUH?
HE COM-FORTED ME WHEN I HAD IT ROUGH...
...MANY TIMES.
ALL THE TIME.
HE ALWAYS HAPPENED TO BE THERE.
YOU WALKED AWAY WITH THE BEST OF EVERY-THING.
AND THE THING IS
KILEY WAS ABLE TO DO ALL THAT BECAUSE I WASN'T PAYING ATTEN-TION.
....

BUT,
I DON'T MIND, MOMO.
I'M GLAD TO SEE THINGS ARE WORKING OUT WITH TOJI. ♡
WHATEVER HE ONCE DID TO HURT YOU,
HE'LL MORE THAN MAKE UP FOR IN THE LONG RUN.
WHEN I LOOKED AT KILEY, WHAT DID I SEE?
HOW DID I MISS IT?
HE WAS ALWAYS THERE FOR ME,
BUT I JUST DIDN'T NOTICE.

.....
IF IT WASN'T FOR YOU,
I MIGHT HAVE DROPPED OUT OF SCHOOL.
THANK YOU...
...KILEY.
I WAS WITH YOU THAT I COULD FORGET MY PAIN.
WHEN TIMES WERE BAD, IT WAS ONLY WHEN
AND..

...IF I HADN'T MET TOJI FIRST, TODAY YOU AND I WOULD PROBABLY BE...

HA HA.
THANKS, MOMO. THAT'S NICE OF YOU TO SAY.
ACK!
OH! AH! MUST RESIST!
...?
I FEEL ANOTHER URGE TO HUG YOU COMING ON.
AND AFTE THAT S XXXXX AND TH SOME OOOOO...
PANT PANT
I BETTER GO NOW, MOMO.
KILEY?
BY THE WAY...
OH, YEAH.

IF YOU EVER GET SICK OF TOJI, GIVE ME A CALL.
I CAN SATISFY PROBLEMS IN BED, TOO. ♡
GO AWAY.

I'M SORRY, KILEY.
AND THANK YOU.
THANK YOU SO MUCH
FOR CARING ABOUT ME.

WHY AM I CRYING?
IT'S NOT LIKE I'LL NEVER SE HIM AGAI
AND YET, I CAN'T STOP THE TEARS.

1-3

MMMMMMMMM

AHEM ...

MOMO ?

CLIC

...

WHAT'S WRONG WITH YOU? YOU KEEP DRIFTING OFF.

OH,

NOTHIN
NOTHIN

IT WOULD BE NICE TO KEEP GOING OUT WITH TOJI, YET HAVE KILEY AROUND
THE WAY IT WAS BEFORE. BUT THAT'S PROBABLY BEING SELFISH.
SOUNDS GOOD.
LOOK, YOUR HAIR'S STANDING UP.
BE-CAUSE YOU KEEP TOUCHING IT.
IT'S MY FAULT?
FIRST OF ALL, NEITHER TOJI NOR KILEY WOULD BE VERY HAPPY WITH THAT ARRANGEMENT.
RATTLE
RATTLE
HUH?
AH, NICE AND COOL.
sniff
sniff

BU-BUMP

OOPS!
STOP!
PUSH

I...
UH...
WHAT DID I JUST DO?
NOT....
GOOD!

ANY GUY'LL GET HURT IF YOU DO THAT TO HIM.
THAT'S NOT GOOD AT ALL!
I SEE...
PEACH GIRL CLUB [part one]
HI, ALL! AND THANKS FOR BUYING PEACH GIRL! I'VE READ THE CARDS AND LETTERS FROM THE READERS WHO'VE ARGUED THAT SAE MIGHT BE JUSTIFIED IN HER ACTIONS, BUT I DON'T KNOW IF I'M CONVINCED.

ONCE IS BAD ENOUGH. BUT TWICE?
WHY DID YOU PULL AWAY FROM HIM?
I DON'T KNOW. HE JUST HAD HIS FACE IN MINE ALL OF A SUDDEN.

I MEAN, UP UNTIL THEN, HE DIDN'T GIVE ME A CLUE!
DON'T I NEED TIME TO GET IN THE MOOD, TOO?

WHAT HAVE YOU GUYS BEEN DOING FOR THE LAST TWO MONTHS?
WAIT! AND THEN WHAT HAPPENED, MOMO?
I GUESS IT REALLY BROUGHT HIM DOWN.
HE DIDN'T EVEN LISTEN TO ME ALL THE WAY HOME.
HMMMPH!

YOU CAN'T LEAVE IT LIKE THAT. YOU'VE GOT TO FIX THINGS BEFORE IT'S TOO LATE.
I GUESS.
BUT HOW DO I DO THAT?
HOW?
COME ON, MOMO...
YOU MUST HAVE *SOME* IDEA.
I HOPE THIS IS FUN FOR YOU ALL!
IT IS! REMINDS ME OF MY FIRST TIME!
COME TO THINK OF IT, I GUESS I WENT THROUGH THAT ONCE MYSELF.
YEAH, ME TOO.
WHEN WAS YOUR FIRST TIME, RIE?
WELL, LET ME THINK...
.....
SNAP
THAT'S IT! I QUIT!

NO, MOMO! WAIT!
I'M LEAVING THE BOOSTER SQUAD! I DON'T HAVE TIME FOR THIS CRAP!
ALL WE EVER DO IS HANG OUT IN THE LOCKER ROOM AND GOSSIP.
BUT WE DON'T PRACTICE OR ANYTHING.
THE CLUB WOULD HAVE TO DISBAND.
YOU CAN'T LEAVE US. WHAT WOULD WE DO WITHOUT YOU?
SINCE THEY'RE JUST A "BOOSTER CLUB" THEY DON'T HAVE THEIR OWN MEETING ROO
IF YOU COULD JUST BE A BIT MOR FLEXIBLE, YOU'D BE LES UPTIGHT ALL THE TIME.
YOU'RE SO BLACK AND WHITE, MOMO. ALMOST LIKE A GUY.
YEAH, IT'S NOT LIKE THE EYES OF THE NATION ARE ON US.
WELL, THAT'S MORE FUN, ISN'T IT?
LIKE NEXT TIME YOU SEE TOJI, WHY DON'T YOU MAKE A MOVE ON HIM?
AND WHOEVER WANTS TO SWIM, CAN SWIM. ♡

OH, ATSU-KO.
TA-KUMA.
I LOVE YOU.
KISS KISS KISS
TOJI.
I LOVE YOU...

I LOVE YOU...
TOJI.
.....
POOF
....
....
OHHHHH!!!
IT'S USELESS! I CAN'T DO THIS!
PITTER PATTER PANT PANT
I WONDER IF TOJI GETS THIS NERVOUS WHEN HE...

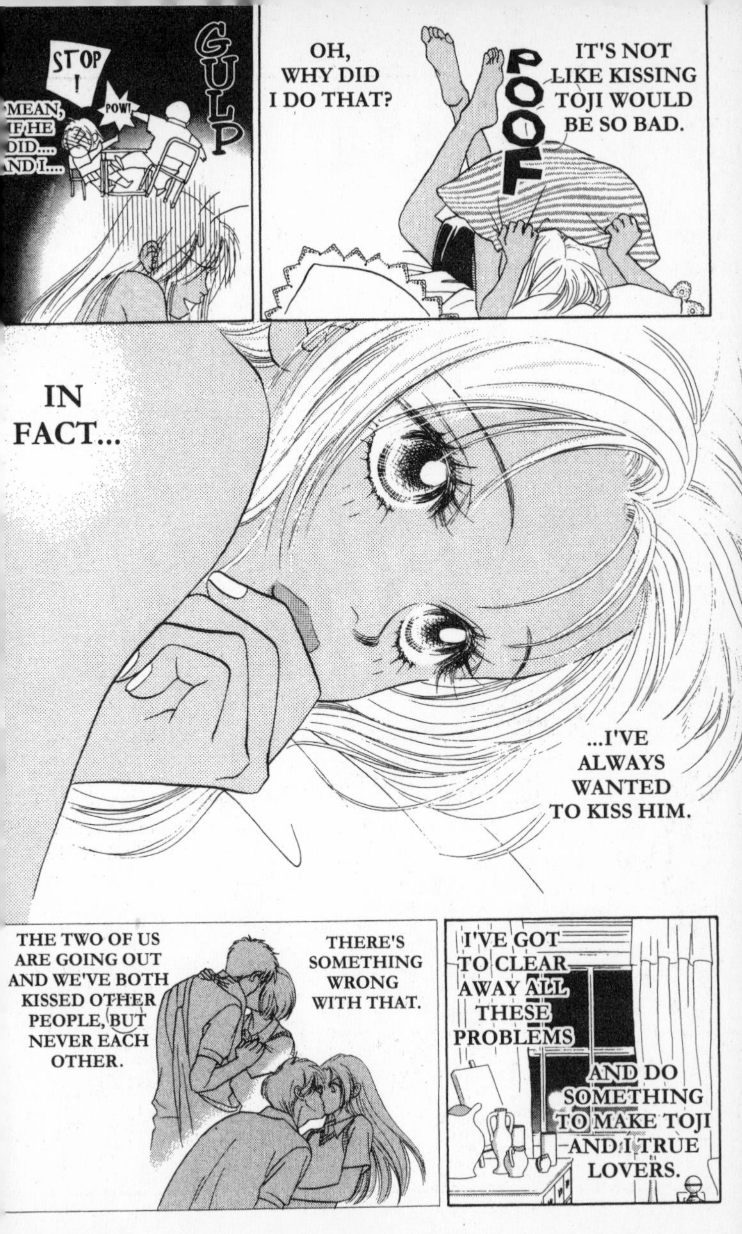
STOP !
POW!
MEAN, IF HE DID... AND I...
GULP
OH, WHY DID I DO THAT?
POOF
IT'S NOT LIKE KISSING TOJI WOULD BE SO BAD.
IN FACT...
...I'VE ALWAYS WANTED TO KISS HIM.
THE TWO OF US ARE GOING OUT AND WE'VE BOTH KISSED OTHER PEOPLE, BUT NEVER EACH OTHER.
THERE'S SOMETHING WRONG WITH THAT.
I'VE GOT TO CLEAR AWAY ALL THESE PROBLEMS
AND DO SOMETHING TO MAKE TOJI AND I TRUE LOVERS.

I REALLY DO WANT ...
...TO KISS HIM.

LOOK OUT!
HERE IT GOES.
YOU'RE GIVING THAT TO TOJI?
HE'S GOING TO LOVE IT!
IT'S BEAUTIFUL!
IT'S INISHED!
HOME MAKING
HOW ARE WE SUPPOSED TO TURN THOSE IN FOR A GRADE?
I DON'T BELIEVE IT!
.....
THEY'RE ALWAYS PICKING ON HER AND TEASING HER.
TODAY SHE'S IN MAYU'S GROUP.
SAE AGAIN.

THAT KIND OF REVENGE ISN'T HEALTHY. IT JUST BRINGS THEM DOWN TO THE SAME LEVEL.
WOW
MOMO, YOU'RE SO RIGHT-EOUS, AREN'T YOU?
WELL, I DO ADMIT, IT'S A LITTLE SATISFYING.
IT DOESN'T MAKE ME FEEL GOOD TO LOOK AT THE POOR THING.

STILL, I DON'T THINK I'M QUITE READY TO COME TO HER RESCUE.
SEE THERE, SAE? IT SERVES YOU RIGHT.
NURSE'S OFFICE
EXCUSE ME?
COULD I GET SOME STOMACH MEDICINE?
COMING RIGHT UP.

MY, YOU GET A LOT OF STOMACH ACHES, DON'T YOU?
HEY, WHAT DO YOU THINK YOU'RE DOING?
NURSE MISAO HAD TO GO OUT. SO I'M HOLDING DOWN THE FORT.
IN THAT GET-UP?
I ALWAYS WANTED TO KNOW HOW IT FELT TO BE A NURSE.
ACTUALLY, I WANTED TO KNOW HOW IT FEELS TO BE IN A NURSE'S CLOTHES!
HERE'S YOUR MEDICINE. ♡
For quick relief from pain associated with PMS
BUFFERON
L
40
PMS?
L SHOW
OU PMS.
IT'S ALRIGHT. THIS WORKS FOR NON-FEMININE PAIN AS WELL. ♡
LIKE PROBLEMS WITH MOMO OR SOMETHING?
SO, FRUSTRATION MAKES IT HURT MORE? YOU SURE STRESS ISN'T AT THE ROOT OF IT ALL?
GULP
TALKING TO YOU IS JUST GIVING ME MORE OF A STOMACH ACHE.
FORGET IT. 'LL FIND SOME IEDICINE MYSELF.

?!
WHAT IS IT? WHEN YOU TRIED TO GET CLOSE TO HER, SHE PUSHED YOU AWAY?
WHAT DO YOU KNOW ABOUT IT?
OOPS. THAT SOUNDS LIKE A BULLS-EYE.
THE WAY YOU MADE THAT GULPING SOUND.
!!!
YOU'RE KIDDING! THAT'S IT?!
SPLISH SLASH
ONE OR TWO THRWARTED ATTEMPTS IS NOTHING.
BUT GETTING BIG KNOTS IN YOUR STOMACH JUST BECAUSE MOMO PUSHED AWAY FROM YOU...
ARE YOU REALLY THAT NAIVE, TOJI?
GULP
GULP

EVERY TIME I TRY ANYTHING SHE FREAKS OUT.
CREAK
DO TELL.
.....
KILEY ...
I BET WHEN YOU TRIED TO KISS HER, SHE DID THE SAME THING. ONLY YOU KEPT GOING, YOU DIRT-BAG!!!

SQUIRT SQUIRT
HAIR GOOD, MAKE-UP IN PLACE.
RUB
LAST NIGH I GAVE MYSE A MUD MAS SO TODAY I'M ALL SET
EVERY-THING'S COMPLETELY READY ...
...FOR WHEN-EVER TOJI GETS HERE!
YOU LIKE SWEETS, DON'T YOU?
I MADE IT FOR YOU IN HOME EC CLASS.
Ta-da!
SURE, I'LL EAT ANYTHING.

..... I'M SORRY ABOUT YESTERDAY.
YOU JUST SURPRISED ME. IT WAS SO SUDDEN.
IT'S NOT LIKE, *YOU KNOW,* I DIDN'T WANT TO.
I SEE.
GREAT. IT'S GOING GREAT.
I JUST HAVE TO SHOW HIM I MEAN IT.
HEY, TOJI. WHY DON'T WE HAVE A SECRET SIGN, JUST BETWEEN US?
A SIGN?
YOU KNOW, LIKE "TIE A YELLOW RIBBON"? OR THAT GUY WHO TAPS HIS BRAKE LIGHT FIVE TIMES WHEN HE'S LEAVING TO TELL HIS GIRL HE LOVES HER.
WHEN WE MAKE AN "L" WITH OUR FINGERS, IT'LL MEAN "I LOVE YOU."
AN "L"?
DING DONG
DING DONG

PING
BUT, AT LEAST...
snicker
RUMBLE RUMBLE
USTLE RUSTLE
ALL SIT
TOO BAD. IT'S TIME.
!
AND WE CAN DO THIS ANYTIME.
I LOVE YOU, TOJI.
I LOVE YOU SQUARED!
COME ON, TOJI! DO IT BACK!

WHAT'S THE PROBLEM? WHY WON'T YOU GIVE ME THE SIGN?
I CAN'T. I JUST CAN'T. IT'S TOO EMBAR-RASSING.
WHAT ARE YOU TALKING ABOUT? IT'S OUR OWN SPECIAL SIGN. NOBODY ELSE KNOWS WHAT IT MEANS.
JUST LIKE IN BASEBALL, YOU HAVE BLOCK SIGNS AND STUFF LIKE THAT, RIGHT?
UT IS IS FFER- NT.
WHAT'S SO DIFFERENT? IT'S EASY. GO ON, TRY IT.
I CAN'T.
COME ON, DO IT.
NO.
DO IT, TOJI!
GRRRRRRRRR
I DON'T WANT TO!!!
PANT
PANT
PANT

I SEE. YOU DON'T WANT TO SAY YOU LOVE ME, IS THAT IT?
NOW THAT I THINK ABOUT IT, YOU HAVEN'T TOLD ME YOU LOVED ME ONCE SINCE WE'VE BEEN GOING OUT.
THAT'S IT, ISN'T IT?
WELL, IT'S NOT THE KIND OF THING THAT'S EASY TO GO AROUND SAYING.
AND WHY NOT?
ALRIGHT,
THEN JUST FORGET IT. YOU OBVIOUSLY DON'T UNDER-STAND ME AT ALL.
THAT'S JUST FINE!

WHAT DOES HE THINK I GO TO ALL THIS TROUBLE FOR?
THAT BLOCK-HEADED DORK.
IF YOU CARE ABOUT ME, CAN'T YOU AT LEAST SAY SO?
EMBAR-ASSED? HAT KIND F LAME EXCUSE S THAT?
COME ON, MOMO. I'LL PAIR UP WITH YOU.
ALRIGHT, GET INTO GROUPS OF TWO TO PRAC-TICE PASSING.
HEY, WATCH OUT!
poit
poont
HOW PATH-ETIC.
LOOK AT SAE. SHE'S THE LONE MAN OUT AGAIN.
TEE HEE HEE

PAM!
HEADS-UP! YOU'RE IN THE WAY!
WHY DON'T YOU GO OVER THERE, WHERE YOU WON'T BOTHER ANYONE?!
flitter flatter
flitter flatter
......
HERE IT GOES.
THROW IT!
ZOOM
HEH HEH HEH
POING
DRIBBLE DRIBBLE
DRIBBLE

ROLLROLLRC
KAPOW
FLOP
SORRY, SAE. DID I HIT YOU?
AH HA HA HA HA HA!
GOT HER!
......

MOMO?
DON'T YOU REMEMBER ME? I'M SAE?
YOU LENT ME YOUR ERASER WHEN WE TOOK THE ENTRANCE EXAM?
WHAT'S THE MATTER? DON'T YOU HAVE A PARTNER?
I'LL TEAM UP WITH YOU.
COME ON. WE CAN PRACTICE OVER THERE.

SORRY, I'LL PASS. WHY DON'T YOU PRACTICE WITH KAKO AND NAMI AND THEM?
HUH?
BOUNCE
BOUNCE
BONK

WE CAN PRACTICE OVER THERE.
FLITTER FLUTTER
swish swish swish

HAVE YOU FORGOTTEN WHAT SHE DID TO YOU?
WHY ARE YOU HELPING SAE?
LET ME ASK YOU THIS. WHEN YOU WERE ALL SO SURE I WAS THE BAD GIRL,
HOW COME EVERY-ONE WAS SO CHUMMY WITH SAE?
....
VELL, WE...
WE HEARD ALL THOSE THINGS SHE WAS SAYING ABOUT YOU.
AND WE FELT SORRY FOR HER.
BUT IF SAE WAS SO TERRIBLE, HOW COULD YOU STAND TO BE FRIENDS WITH HER?
AE'S NOT URE EVIL.
YOU HAD SOME GOOD TIMES WHEN YOU WERE HANGING OUT WITH HER, DIDN'T YOU?
BUT, I DON'T WANT TO BE RE-SPON-SIBLE...
...IF SHE TURNS EVERY-ONE AGAINST YOU AGAIN.
THANKS FOR WOR-RYING ABOUT ME.
I'M SURE IT'LL BE OKAY.

HO AR YO TOD ?
GOOD MORNING, MOMO!
AFTER ALL, NOW SAE'S PROBABLY LEARNED A LITTLE ABOUT HOW IT FEELS TO BE THE OUTCAST.
I'LL CLEAN THEM FOR YO RIGHT AWAY.
THEY'RE JUST A BIT DIRTY.
PAT
PAT
BRUSH
BRUSH
dust
dust
YOUR INDOOR SHOES ARE RIGHT HERE.
HERE, LET ME TAKE YOUR BAG FOR YOU.
WHAT IS IT, MOMO? SOMETHING I CAN D FOR YOU
RIGHT HERE
SAE.
WHATEVER YOU SA MOMO YOUR WISH I MY CO MAND
I FEEL LIKE I'M YOUR BOSS OR SOMETHING.
CAN'T YOU JUST BE NORMAL?
...
IT'S ALMOST CREEPY.
D-DID YOU SEE THAT? TALK ABOUT A 180°.
WOW

Squeak
1-3

HI, MOMO. I--

HMMMPH

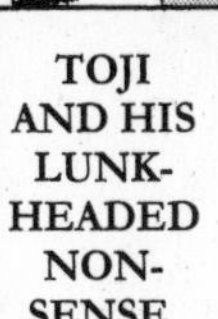
TOJI AND HIS LUNK-HEADED NON-SENSE.
I DON'T EVEN FEEL LIKE LISTENING TO WHAT-EVER HE HAS TO SAY.

MOMO, ARE YOU HAVING A FIGHT WITH TOJI? IS THERE ANYTHING I CAN DO TO HELP?

YEAH! STAY OUT OF IT.

I DON'T WANT TO WASTE MY TIME WITH HIM.

ALRIGHT, NEXT LET'S HAVE OGAWA, YAMADA, AND TOJIGAMORI COME TO THE FRONT OF THE CLASS.
OWWWWW
my stomach
under his desk
....
OH, GREAT.
THINK I'M GOING TO BE IN TROUBLE.
RUSTLE
SQUEAK
CLUNK
I GUESS I'VE KNOWN IT ALL ALONG.
TOJI'S THE EASY-GOING TYPE THAT HAS TROUBLE SAYING SERIOUS STUFF LIKE "I LOVE YOU."

IT WOULD MEAN SO MUCH.
BUT IF HE'D JUST SAY IT ONE TIME.
I KNOW YOU CAN'T MAKE A LEOPARD CHANGE HIS SPOTS, BUT I JUST WISH...
WHAT'S THE MATTER, TOJI? YOU DON'T GET IT?
SIGH
.....
!!

I SEE. GOOD JOB. YOU CAN SIT DOWN NOW.
CLINK
NO, I'M UH...
ALRIGHT, LET'S TAKE THE PROBLEMS FROM THE FAR LEFT.
IT'S POINT-LESS TO TRY AND MAKE HIM DO THINGS AGAINST HIS WILL.
I GUESS I'LL HAVE TO TALK TO HIM LATER.
YOU CAN SIT DOWN NOW.
HUH? TOJI? YOU'RE STILL THERE?

WHIRL
HUH?
WHAT'S HE DOING?
HE'S TURNED INTO A STATUE

mumble
mumble
hisper
hisper
BOING

NOW, TAKE YOUR SEAT.
CLONK
REAL FUNNY, KNUCKLE-HEAD!
HA HA HA HA HA

WHAT ARE YOU DOING? RUNNING FOR PRESIDENT?
WHAT WERE YOU DOING, TOJI? WHAT WAS THE MEANING OF THAT?

I'M SORRY, TOJI.
THAT MUST HAVE BEEN EMBAR-RASSING.
IT WASN'T REALLY THAT BAD.
NOT REALLY.
WELL, MAYBE A LITTLE AT FIRST, BUT ONCE I GOT INTO IT...
THANK YOU.
I WAS REALLY HAPPY, TOJI.

MOMO! I DIDN'T WANT YOU TO WORRY!
SLIP
THU

SO, I BROUGHT YOU YOUR BOOKS FROM THE CLASS-ROOM!
HERE THEY ARE, MOMO.
THERE, YOU'VE GOT THEM.
YOUR NEXT CLASS IS IN THE SCIENCE LAB. JUST SO YOU WON'T FORGET.
WE WERE ALMOST... THE MOOD WAS PER-FECT...
I DON'T BELIEVE IT.
MOMO?
....
WELL, I'LL SEE YOU THERE.
I SHOULD NEVER HAVE HELPED HER!

W-W-W-
WOW!♡

I UNDERSTAND IT'S YOUR BIRTHDAY SOON, ISN'T THAT RIGHT, MOMO?
IS THERE ANYTHING I CAN BUY YOU AS A PRESENT?
WHAT? NO, DON'T WORRY ABOUT IT.
PLEASE, MOMO, DON'T BE AFRAID TO ASK.
MOMO?
EXCUSE US, YOU WITH THE TAN.

THOSE ARE BEAUTIFUL SHOES.
WHERE'D YOU GET THEM?

THEY GO GREAT WITH YOUR SCHOOL CLOTHES.

HOW HIGH'S THE HEEL? TWO INCHES? NO, GOT TO BE FOUR INCHES.

EXCUSE ME!

!!

A CAMERA!

THESE GUYS AREN'T...?

THEY'RE NOT PERVERTS, ARE THEY?

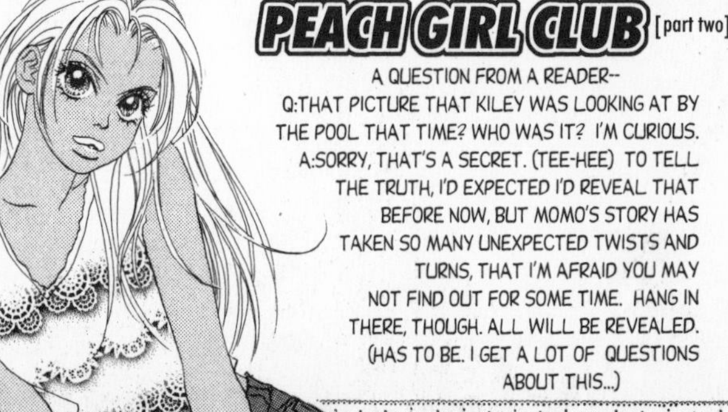

PEACH GIRL CLUB [part two]

A QUESTION FROM A READER--

Q:THAT PICTURE THAT KILEY WAS LOOKING AT BY THE POOL THAT TIME? WHO WAS IT? I'M CURIOUS.

A:SORRY, THAT'S A SECRET. (TEE-HEE) TO TELL THE TRUTH, I'D EXPECTED I'D REVEAL THAT BEFORE NOW, BUT MOMO'S STORY HAS TAKEN SO MANY UNEXPECTED TWISTS AND TURNS, THAT I'M AFRAID YOU MAY NOT FIND OUT FOR SOME TIME. HANG IN THERE, THOUGH. ALL WILL BE REVEALED. (HAS TO BE. I GET A LOT OF QUESTIONS ABOUT THIS...)

LET'S GET OUT OF HERE, SAE!
WE'RE, UH, WITH THIS COMPANY...
Men's Monthly
Editorial Staff Yukitoshi Honda
The Danron Corporation
3-2-18 Bunkyo-ward, Tokyo 112
Phone 5395-34XX
Fax 5943-91XX
MEN'S MONTHLY??
YOU MAY HAVE HEARD OF US. SOME OF YOUR BETTER KNOWN POP IDOLS LIKE MATSUNOUCHI AND TABENA GOT THEIR START WITH OUR MAGAZINE.
NO WAY! I LOVE BOTH THOSE GUYS! WHOA!
WE'RE OUT WORKING ON A NEW ARTICLE...
AND TODAY WE'RE LOOKING FOR FASHIONABLY DRESSED HIGH SCHOOL GIRLS FOR A STORY WE'RE DOING.
AND AS I SAID, THOSE SHOES ARE REALLY STYLISH.
I'VE ALWAYS THOUGHT THAT A LITTLE HEEL MAKES MY LEGS SEEM MUCH LONGER AND SO...
UH HUH. GO ON.
I THOUGHT SO, TOO. THE VERY FIRST TIME THEY CAUGHT MY EYE AT THE SHOE STORE.
I SEE. INTEREST ING.

DO YOU THINK WE COULD GET A PICTURE?
REALLY?
BUT I DON'T THINK I PHOTOGRAPH ALL THAT WELL.
DON'T WORRY. WE'LL TAKE A LOT OF SHOTS AND USE THE BEST ONE.
THIS GUY'S A REAL PRO.
HEY!
HOW ABOUT THESE?
KER-KLUNK
FRIEND OF YOURS?
WELL,
YEAH,
SHE'S WITH ME.
I... UH ...
YES, I AM !
ALL READY TO GET PHOTOGRAPHED.
THAT'S RIGHT.

COULD YOU STRIKE A POSE OR SOME-THING.
SOME-THING ABOUT YOUR LOOK. IT'S WELL... FLAT.
A GHOS
CLI-CLICK
A MUF-FLER.
CLI-CLICK
A PUSH-UP BRA.
CLI-CLICK
GULP

ARE YOU SERIOUS?!!
MEN'S MON-THLY?!
I WISH I'D WALKED HOME WITH YOU!
YOU'RE SO LUCKY!
WHEN'S IT COMING OUT?
THE FIRST OF NEXT MONTH.
HOW DID IT FEEL TO GET PHOTO-GRAPHED LIKE THAT?
I DON'T KNOW. I KIND OF WISH I HADN'T DONE IT.
I WAS JUST SO FLATTERED WHEN THESE PROFESSIONAL GUYS STARTED PRAISING MY SHOES.
?
YOU SURE THE SHOES WERE ALL THEY WERE PRAISING?
PiKPiKi
HEY, EVERYONE, THEY PRAISED ME TOO. DIDN'T THEY, MOMO?
T-EE HEE HEE HEE HEE
WHAT'S THAT SUPPOSED TO MEAN?
TELL US ABOUT THE EDITOR GUY. WAS HE GOOD LOOKING?
NO RESPONSE.

HEY GU
YOU WA
TO HEA
SOME
THING
THE MONTHLY HEART THROB. IT'S WHAT *MEN'S MONTHLY* IS FAMOUS FOR.
"BOY TOYS?"
OF COURSE. THE BOY TOYS AREN'T GOING TO COME OUT TO TAKE PICTURES OF SHOES.
SO HE WASN'T ON PAR WITH THEIR MODELS?
HEY EVERY-ONE. GUESS WHAT?
NOT REALLY.
MEN'S MONTHLY HEARTTHROB OF THE MONTH GORO OOJI (19) NUMBER ONE MODEL
WELL, HE'S SO BEAUTI-FUL, I'D FORGIVE HIM.
IS IT TRUE THESE GUYS BRING A DIFFERENT GIRL HOME EVERY NIGHT?
THEY DON'T REALLY, DO THEY?
A LOT OF THESE MODELS MUST BE REAL STUCK UP.
UH... HEY.....
ONE TIME WOULD BE ENOUGH. I'D JUST LOVE TO SEE A REAL MODEL.

OH, MOMO!
SAE, I'VE GOT MY BOOSTER CLUB TO-DAY, SO YOU CAN GO ON AHEAD.
WHEN *MEN'S MONTHLY* COMES OUT WE'RE ALL GOING TO BUY IT.♡
CONGRAT-ULATIONS ON YOUR MODELING DEBUT.
WE JUST RAN INTO HER IN THE HALL.
KAKO DID.
WHAT'S THAT? WHO TOLD YOU?
?!
LOOK, IT WASN'T A MODELING DEBUT, OKAY? DON'T START SAYING ALL KINDS OF STUFF.

SCHOOL BEAUTIFICATION COMMITTEE THIS MONTH'S AGENDA

I FEEL LIKE

THEY'RE ALL JUST USING ME.

THEY DON'T CARE ABOUT ME. THEY JUST DON'T WANT THEIR

BOOSTER CLUB TO GET KICKED OUT OF THE LOCKER ROOM.

EVEN SO, YOU HAVE FUN HANGING OUT WITH THEM, DON'T YOU?

YEAH

I LIKE THE CLUB ACTIVITIES. BUT EVEN MORE THAN THAT, I LIKE JUST COM-ING TO SCHOOL.
I HAVE FUN.
A FEW MONTHS AGO I'D NEVER HAVE THOUGHT...
MY DARLING TOJI...
I HAVE FRIENDS WHO UNDER-STAND ME...
...I'D BE SO HAPPY.
IF WE HURRY, WE JUST MIGHT.
THINK WE'LL MAKE IT?
SHOOT, WE'RE GOING TO BE LATE.
THAT TEACHER JUST NEVER STOPS TALKING.
MOMO, WAIT FOR ME!!

FLITTER FLITTER FLITTER
!!
SAE? I TOLD YOU TO GO AHEAD.
I DIDN'T MIND WAITING. NOTHING TO DO ANYWAY.
......
HERE, MOMO. I BROUGHT YOU YOUR BAG.
THERE'RE ONLY TWO OF THEM.
...
WELL, SOMEONE GAVE TOJI THESE MOVIE TICKETS.
OH... I...UH...
DID YOU TWO HAVE A DATE?
I DON'T...
WHAT ARE YOU GOING TO DO?
WELL, YOU TWO CAN GO.
WE DON'T HAVE TO GO.
BUT THEY'RE YOUR TICKETS.
BUT THESE ARE ONLY GOOD UNTIL TODAY.

I GUESS WE COULD BUY ONE MORE AND SPLIT IT THREE WAYS.
I WON'T HEAR OF IT!!!
BESIDES, I JUST REMEM-BERED,
I HAVE SOMETHING ELSE TO DO. I'M BUSY. YOU TWO GO. AND HAVE A GOOD TIME.
BUT WE--
GO, GO. PLEASE.
....
HAVE FUN YOU TWO.
VELL IANKS, SAE.
I'LL MAKE IT UP TO YOU LATER.

......
BBBBBRRRRRRRRRRRRRRRRRRRRR
THOSE WERE THE DAYS...
HEY, THERE!
HI, SAE!
YO, SAE!
SAE, HOW ARE YOU?
SNAP!
HUH!

SMASH
OW OW
MO MO
MO MO
KICK
KICK
STOMP
STOMP
THAT...
THAT...
THAT...
THAT...
THAT...
MOMO!
KICK
KICK
STOMP
STOMP
KA-POW!!!
YEAH, SHE OBVIOUSLY DIDN'T HAVE ANY OTHER PLANS.
I KNOW.
I THOUGHT FOR SURE SHE WAS GOING TO TAG ALONG.
I HOPE SAE WASN'T TOO UPSET.
Titanic

WHEN SAE CHANGES, SHE REALLY CHANGES.
CLUNK
AHHHHH
WHEW

LOOK AT MY SHOES!
SAE, YOU DID THIS, DIDN'T YOU?
I KNEW SHE'D NEVER CHANGE. YOU'RE OUT OF THE GROUP!
....
UH OH

IS THAT? COULD IT REALLY BE? MY PHONE?
IT'S BEEN SO LONG SINCE ANYONE CALLED.
YUCK. ALL THESE COBWEBS.

SO I GOT YOU THIS PRESENT.
SAE, I FELT BAD ABOUT YESTER-DAY.
YOU ONCE TOLD ME YOU LIKE THOSE COOKIES THEY SELL BY THE STATION.
OH, HOW SWEET.

WELL, YEAH...
?
REMEMBER HOW YESTERDAY YOU SAID YOU'D MAKE IT UP TO ME?
YOU CAN DO THAT BY GOING SOMEWHERE WITH ME AFTER SCHOOL TODAY.
THE PHOTO STUDIO
SHE LOOKS EVEN BETTER IN PERSON!
SHE'S ADORABLE!
SHE'S SO TINY!
WOW! LOOK!
IS THIS SAE?
COME ON, EVERYONE. GIV HER SOME ROO WE DON'T WANT TO SCAR HER AWAY.
WHY, SHE WON'T EVEN NEED ANY MAKE-UP!
ESPECIALLY COMPARED TO HER FRIEND.
IT AL-MOST GLOWS!
LOOK HOW SOFT AND WHITE HER SKIN IS!
AND YOU'RE ONLY 15? INCREDIBLE!

THANK YOU AGAIN FOR YESTERDAY, MR. HONDA.
NO PROBLEM.
THANK YOU FOR COMING.
SAY, AREN'T YOU THE GIRL FROM...
I JUST BROUGHT HER ALONG AS A CHAPERONE.
OH, I SEE.
OKAY, WELL LET'S CHANGE YOUR CLOTHES AND FIX YOUR HAIR.
WE'VE GOT A BUSY AFTERNOON AHEAD.
YES SIR! ♡
WHAT IN THE HECK IS GOING ON?
S-SAE? WHERE ARE YOU--?
OH, SORRY, MOMO. YOU DON'T MIND WAITING HERE, DO YOU?
THE NERVE! SHE DRAGS ME HERE AND THEN DITCHES ME!
BUT SAE!

MEN'S MONTHLY ISSUE NUMBER 19
HELP US FIND OUR MEN'S MONTHLY GIRLFRIEND!
All entrants must be between 13 and 20 years of age.
There are no physical requirements.
Winner to be announced on September 23rd!!!!
JOIN NOW!
THE MEN'S MONTHLY GIRLFRIEND?
THAT'S WHAT WE WERE GOING ALL OVER TOWN TAKING PICTURES FOR.
LIKE THIS.
WE'RE GOING TO LET OUR READERS PICK THEIR FAVORITE GIRL.
WE'RE NOT JUST LOOKING FOR CUTE GIRLS,
BUT GIRLS WITH A DISTINCTIVE FLAIR. SAE'S A PERFECT CANDIDATE.
SAE JUST WANTED ME TO SEE ALL THIS.
SHE'S STI GOT HE HIDDEN AGENDA I GUESS THAT PA HASN'T CHANGE
NOW I GET IT.
I BET SHE'S REALLY POPULAR AT SCHOOL TOO, ISN'T SHE?
SHE SURE IS.

Studio 2
GLI-CLICK
GLI-CLICK
BEAUTIFUL. MARVELOUS.
THAT'LL TICKLE THE HORMONES.
OHHHHHH GOROOOOOO
WHENEVER GORO'S UP FOR A PHOTO SHOOT, THEY ALWAYS SEEM TO KNOW. AND THERE'S MORE EVERY TIME.
YOU'RE NOT KIDDING. LOOK AT THAT MOB OUT THERE.
THANKS.
A TOWEL FOR YOUR FACE, GORO.
GORO, WOULD YOU LIKE A DRINK?
THANKS, GORO.
GORROOOOOO
THAT'S A WRAP.

I COULD JUST DIE !!!!!
HE SAID THANKS!!!
OHHHHH!
UNBELIEVABLE THAT A GUY LIKE THAT ONLY HAS ONE GIRLFRIEND.
YOU THINK HE'S GAY?
JUST WAIT. YOU THINK THE FANS ARE BAD NOW.
IS IT TRUE HE'S GOING TO BE ON A TV SHOW?
THAT'S WHY HE'S OUR NUMBER ONE MODEL.
TALK ABOUT TICKLING HORMONES. THAT GUY'S GOT SEX APPEAL OOZING FROM HIM.
AFTER A WHILE, HE JUST WANTS AN EVERYDAY, NORMAL GIRL.
A GUY LIKE THAT GETS TIRED OF BEING PURSUED BY ALL THE BIG FISH.

PITTER PATTER
BUMP
AH!
ROLL ROLL
ROLL
HUH?
OOF
OH, MY BACK.
HMM?
I'M SORRY. LET ME HELP YOU.
I HARDLY EVEN TOUCHED HER.
ARE YOU ALRIGHT?
ITTER
!

OH.
THAN
YOU
......
OH!
COULD YOU PUT ME DOWN PLEASE?
YES,
SIR.
HEY SAE. ARE YOU READY?

HEY, MR. HONDA.
WHO WAS THAT?
OH,
THAT'S ONE OF OUR *MEN'S MONTHLY* GIRLFRIEND CANDIDATES. HER NAME'S SAE.
CUTE, ISN'T SHE?
SO MANY HANDSOME MEN AROUND THE STUDIO.
I WONDER IF HE'S A MODEL?
TEE HEE HEE
I'LL HAVE TO BE CAREFUL.
IT'S NO PROBLEM.
I'M SORRY.
FLUTTER
.....
HOW LONG IS THIS GOING TO TAKE?
YAWN
BUT LOOK THIS WAY.
OKAY,
MOVE AROUND.
AND LIGHT. VERY LIGHT.

WILL YOU LOOK AT THE TIME.
!!
AND MOM'S GOING TO BE LATE TONIGHT SO I'M SUPPOSED TO COOK DINNER.
CLI -CLICK
WHO
T'S
GORO, THE MONTHLY HEARTTHROB!
WHE
NO, THANK YOU.
THANKS, SAE.
OKAY, THAT'S A WRAP.
THAT'S UNUSUAL. HE USUALLY DOESN'T HANG AROUND AND WATCH.
HE'S SO HOT!
IT'S REALLY HIM !!!
HEY, CHECK IT OUT. GORO'S STILL HERE.

GREAT, NOW WE CAN GO.
SAE?
EVERYBODY, I MADE YOU ALL SOME COOKIES. HAVE A FEW.
WHAT?!?!?!
THANK YOU.
HERE'S SOME TEA TO WASH THEM DOWN WITH.
MMM. THEY'RE GOOD.
THOSE ARE THE COOKIES THAT I BOUGHT BECAUSE I FELT SORRY FOR HER.
THAT WITCH!
THESE COOKIES TASTE PROFES-SIONALLY BAKED.
AMAZING, SAE. YOU'RE REALLY MULTI-TALENTED.
HEY, SAE. DO YOU THINK WE CAN GET SOME SHOTS OF YOU IN YOUR SCHOOL CLOTHES BEFORE YOU GO?
SURE.
UH, SAE?
I'M SORRY, BUT I GOT TO GET HOME. I'LL SEE YOU TOMORROW.
?!

NO! MOMO! YOU CAN'T GO! PLEASE, STAY JUST A LITTLE LONGER. I'M ALMOST FINISHED.
LOOK, YOU BROUGHT ME HERE TO SEE ALL THIS AND I SAW IT.
AREN'T YOU SATISFIEI
PLEASE, MOMO.
WITHOUT SOMEONE WITH ME, I FEEL SO SMALL.
SOMETHING'S WRONG WITH THIS GIRL.
THE W MOM LOOKS EVERYO ELSE
PLEASE MOMO. JUST RELAX.
JUST A FEW MORE MINUTES.
WELL, HURRY IT UP!
YES, MOMO. I'M HURRYING.
....

WHY DO YOU KEEP KISSING UP TO HER?
WHO DOES SHE THINK SHE IS?
AREN'T YOU THE GUY THAT JUST --?

LOOK AT HER. SITTING OVER THERE LIKE SHE RULES THE WORLD.

HUH?

I'M SORRY.

IT'S NONE OF MY BUSINESS.

I JUST MET YOU. I SHOULDN'T BE INSULTING YOUR FRIEND.

I APOLOGIZE.

NO, NO. YOU'RE RIGHT. THANK YOU FOR NOTICING.
ALL I EVER DO IS KOWTOW TO MOMO. IT'S MADE MY LIFE UNBEARABLE.
IT'S BECAUSE OF HER THAT I'M MISERABLE AND HATE GOING TO SCHOOL.

EVEN TODAY. I DIDN'T WANT HER TO COME, BUT SHE INSISTED. AND NOW ALL SHE'S DOING IS PUTTING PRESSURE ON ME.

WHAT A LOUSE.
I BET SHE'S JUST JEALOUS BECAUSE SHE'S NOT AS CUTE AS YOU.

ER...
I...
HO HO HO HO HO
YOU'RE TELLING US
THAT HE SAID HE'S NEVER SEEN A GIRL AS PRETTY AS YOU?
I DON'T BELIEVE IT.

HE WAS JUST TAKEN WITH ME FOR SOME REASON.

HE ASKED IF HE COULD SEE ME AGAIN. ♡

YOU SURE YOU'RE TALKING ABOUT A *MEN'S MONTHLY* MODEL?

AND NOT A CAMERA MAN THAT FED YOU SOME LINE?

YEAH, IF HE WAS SO IN LOVE WITH YOU, YOU COULD HAVE AT LEAST GOT HIS NAME AND NUMBER.

IT'S TRUE. IT'S ALL TRUE.

OKAY, THEN WHO IS HE?

IF YOU DON'T KNOW HIS NAME, JUST POINT TO HIS PICTURE.

PLOP

HIM.

THIS IS THE GUY.

MEN'S MONTHLY
THE FASHION MAGAZINE
10
OCTOBER ISSUE
CHOOSING THE RIGHT COAT FOR THE RIGHT OCCASION
HOT HAIR FOR THE COOLER WEATHER
WHY RED WINE IS BETTER
100 OF THE BEST PLACES TO PARADE IN PARIS
SUITABLE SUITS

POIT

WHOOOSH
Men's Monthly
10
CHOOSING THE RIGHT COAT FOR THE RIGHT OCCASION
100 OF THE BEST PLACES
SUITABLE SUITS
AT LEAST MAKE YOUR LIES CONCEIV-ABLE!!!
HA HA HA HA HA HA HA
NOT JUST A MODEL. NOW IT'S THE HEARTHROB OF THE MONTH!
YEAH, RIGHT! GIVE ME A BREAK!
GO AWAY, SAE. WE'VE GOT REAL THINGS TO TALK ABOUT.
GRRRRRR
IT'S NOT A LIE!
IT'S THE TRUTH!

YOU ALWAYS WANT TO BE THE CENTER OF ATTENTION.
BUT IF YOU KEEP LYING ALL THE TIME,
NO ONE WILL EVER BELIEVE YOU AGAIN.

UNDER-STAND?
POP

HISSSSSSSSSSSS

FLITTER
FLATTER
FLUTTER

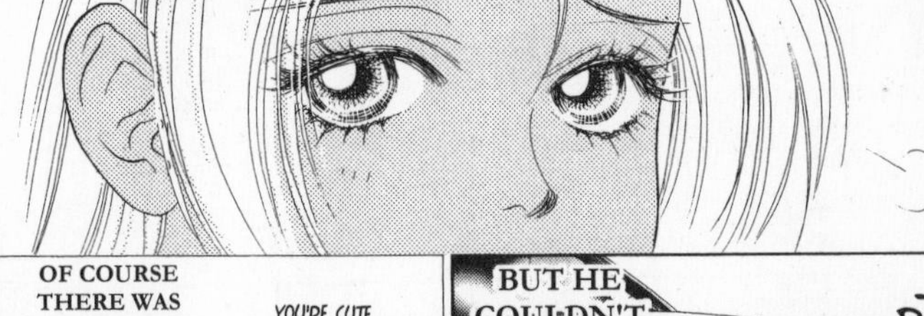

OF COURSE THERE WAS ONE OF THOSE MODELS IN THE STUDIO YESTERDAY.
YOU'RE CUTE, AREN'T YOU BABE? YOU WANT TO GET TOGETHER SOME TIME?
GEE

BUT HE COULDN'T HAVE...
RRRTTT
...COULD HE?

SLAM
JUST A MINUTE, YOUNG MAN.
WHERE DO YOU THINK YOU'RE GOING?
THIS CAMPUS IS CLOSED TO VISITORS. ONLY STUDENTS AND FACULTY
ARE...
whirl
KA-BOING

KA-KLUNK
HEY YOU! WHO DO YOU THINK YOU'RE--
!!
MS. MARU-YAMA ?
KA-KLANK
KA-POW
KA-BOOM
NO ONE IS IMMUNE.
WRITE "I'M A BIG LIAR AND AN IDIOT!" DO IT!
NOW PUT IT ON THE WALL THERE!
LET GO! WHAT ARE YOU DOING?!
WE'RE TIRED OF YOUR RIDICULOUS LIES! YOU AND THAT FAMOUS MODEL! IT'S TOO MUCH!

SMACK
HISSSS
HERE. IF YOU CAN'T DO IT YOURSELF, WE'LL HELP YOU.
I'M SORRY. PLEASE. I'M SORRY.
WHAT WAS THAT? WE DIDN'T HEAR.
HURRY UP! WE'RE WAITING!
!!!
WHIRL
HISSSSSSSSS
WHAT DO YOU THIN YOU'R DOIN ?!
YUCK! IT'S ALL OVER!
YOU HAG!
OH!
AG!
HISSSSS

A MODEL? AT OUR SCHOOL?
COME DOWN HERE AND LOOK AT THIS!

I DON'T BELIEVE IT!
OUT OF THE WAY! LET ME SEE!
IS! IT'S HIM!
YOU?
WHAT ARE YOU...?
I COULDN'T STOP THINKING ABOUT YOU, SAE.

I THINK...
...I WANT TO BE WITH YOU!

TO BE CONTINUED IN PEACH GIRL 5

Momo's finally dating the man of her dreams, and she's gained popularity at school. After feeling a little deflated, Sae's finally back into shape when the hottest model from *Men's Monthly Magazine* confesses his love for her. Now with a new man on her arm and a chance to become a famous supermodel, Sae is back in the limelight. But, she won't be completely satisfied until she shatters Momo's happiness and snatches Toji for herself. Sae's got a new plan, even more wicked and devious than her last, to break up the happy couple for good. Be sure to check out what happens next in *Peach Girl 5*!